Being a Good Teammate

Katie Peters

GRL Consultants,
Diane Craig and Monica Marx,
Certified Literacy Specialists

Lerner Publications ◆ Minneapolis

Note from a GRL Consultant
This Pull Ahead leveled book has been carefully designed for beginning readers. A team of guided reading literacy experts has reviewed and leveled the book to ensure readers pull ahead and experience success.

Copyright © 2022 by Lerner Publishing Group, Inc.

All rights reserved. International copyright secured. No part of this book may be reproduced, stored in a retrieval system, or transmitted in any form or by any means—electronic, mechanical, photocopying, recording, or otherwise—without the prior written permission of Lerner Publishing Group, Inc., except for the inclusion of brief quotations in an acknowledged review.

Lerner Publications Company
An imprint of Lerner Publishing Group, Inc.
241 First Avenue North
Minneapolis, MN 55401 USA

For reading levels and more information, look up this title at www.lernerbooks.com.

Main body text set in Memphis Pro 24/39
Typeface provided by Linotype

Photo Acknowledgments
The images in this book are used with the permission of: © FatCamera/Getty Images, pp. 6–7, 12–13; © ilbusca/Getty Images, p. 3; © Jupiterimages/Getty Images, pp. 10–11, 16 (left); © kali9/Getty Images, pp. 4–5, 16 (center); © SDI Productions/Getty Images, pp. 8–9, 16 (right); © Thomas Barwick/Getty Images, pp. 14–15.

Front cover: © FatCamera/Getty Images.

Library of Congress Cataloging-in-Publication Data

Names: Peters, Katie, author.
Title: Being a good teammate / Katie Peters.
Description: Minneapolis : Lerner Publications, 2022. | Series: Be a good sport. Pull ahead readers. People smarts, Nonfiction | Includes bibliographical references and index. | Audience: Ages 4–7 | Audience: Grades K–1 | Summary: "See what it means to play on a team. Practice, play, win, and lose with your teammates. Pairs with the fiction title Reiko's Team"— Provided by publisher.
Identifiers: LCCN 2021010372 (print) | LCCN 2021010373 (ebook) | ISBN 9781728440934 (library binding) | ISBN 9781728444413 (ebook)
Subjects: LCSH: Teamwork (Sports)—Juvenile literature. | Sportsmanship—Juvenile literature.
Classification: LCC GV706.8 .P46 2022 (print) | LCC GV706.8 (ebook) | DDC 796—dc23

LC record available at https://lccn.loc.gov/2021010372
LC ebook record available at https://lccn.loc.gov/2021010373

Manufactured in the United States of America
3-1009732-49708-5/31/2023

Table of Contents

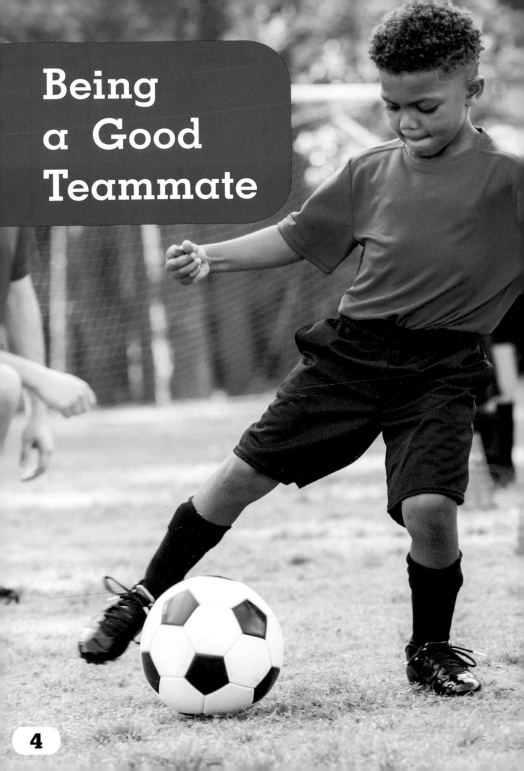

Being a Good Teammate

I practice with my
teammates.

I play with my teammates.

I win with my teammates.

I lose with my teammates.

I cheer with my teammates.

My teammates are fun!

Can you think of a time when you were a good teammate?

Did You See It?

coach

cone

cup

Index